Francesco Roncalli

VATICAN CITY

MONUMENTI, MUSEI E GALLERIE PONTIFICIE

CONTENTS

The photographs of the Sistine Chapel frescoes after cleaning are reproduced by courtesy of NTV - Tokyo

© Copyright 1989 by Gestione Vendita Pubblicazioni, Città del Vaticano and SCALA, Istituto Fotografico Editoriale, Antella (Firenze)
Photographs SCALA (M. Sarri, M. Falsini, N. Grifoni, A. Corsini) except: 7, 76, 78, 81 (Vatican Museums; P. Zigrossi); 17-24 and 35 (Bruno Del Priore); 43 (Servizio fotografico dell'Osservatore Romano; A. Mari); 64 (Alinari); 151 and cover (Pubbliaerfoto)
Lay-out: Daniele Casalino
Translation: Mary Jo Meade
Produced by SCALA
Printed by Tipografia Poliglotta Vaticana, 1989

Front cover: Aerial view of St. Peter's Square

Frontispiece: View of S. Peter's Dome from the Aventine

1. St. Peter's Basilica

On page 128: Michelangelo, the Papal Coat of arms in the Sistine Chapel

Back cover: The swearing ceremony of the Swiss Guard in the St. Damasus Courtyard

THE BASILICA OF ST. PETER

"When you were young, you girded yourself and walked where you would; but when you are old, you stretch out your hands, and another girds you and carries you where you do not wish to go" (Jn. 21:18).

Before the eyes of whoever—pilgrim, scholar or tourist—visits this place, this monument and the buildings, which have multiplied over the centuries, are the historical evidence of Christ's prophecy. Christ's prophecy pinpointed not only the place, time and mode of Peter's martyrdom, but also the hard ground on which that simple testimony would be realized and transformed. Christ's words are constantly being tested, and there is not always a victorious result on the human level.

In 313 A.D. an imperial rescript, commonly known as the Edict of Milan, acknowledged the Christians' right to religious freedom and restored to their cult places which had previously been confiscated. Between 320 and 350 A.D. there rose a great church on the grave of Peter the apostle; in

2. The obelisk in the center of the square   *3. St. Peter's Square and Via della Conciliazione from the dome*

order to erect this edifice, an entire burial ground, which had been expanding on the slopes of the Vatican Hill near Nero's and Caligula's Circus, was covered and levelled.

The pilgrim or tourist who today arrives in this square has difficulty imagining the period during which the small homes of the guards, shelters for pilgrims and those lodgings (dating from the 5th century) given to the Pope, resident of the Lateran, so that he might stay overnight for the liturgical celebrations, neighbored the then recently-erected basilica. All so very modest and precarious that the simple dripping of rain water from the roof of the basilica caused these buildings serious damage!

It was not until the Jubilee of 1600 that the pilgrims saw, for the first time, the dome of the new church which was triumphantly enlarged, crowned by a bronze ball and a cross, blessed by Clement VIII in 1597. Fifteen years later Carlo Maderno finished the façade, enlarging it, thereby seeking to restore che concept of unity to the controversial architectural growth of the temple edifice. From that time until the present, the complex place which we today call the Vatican created, with a density directly proportionate to the proximity of St. Peter's Tomb, many of the fundamental pages of the history of Christianity, of the Church, of the Papacy and of Western Culture. In the architecture and the works of art, sometimes used as symbols, sometimes as mere glitter, the real story of the cult is revealed; also revealed is the fact that religious piety, on the one hand, and worldliness, on the other, were inextricably mixed. The architecture and the art, their images recorded in this album, create a partial but certainly a faithful impression of the phenomenal historical events of the Church.

"Whoever you are, you that seek the names of both Peter and Paul. . ."; thus Pope Damaso, in the 4th century, addressed the pilgrims in a location on the Appian Way, dedicated to the memory of both apostles. Both martyred in Rome between 64 and 67 A.D., one buried in the Vatican and the other along Via Ostiense. Peter and Paul met one another, for the first time, in Jerusalem in 39 A.D. At that time the young Christian community was still sceptical of Saul's recent conversion. "And I remained with him (Peter) for fifteen days", Paul later recounted to the Galatians (1:18). About ten

years later, they saw one another and decided to divide their tasks between them: Peter chose to attend to those Christians originating from Judaism while Paul chose to attend to those originating from Paganism. Paul, later to be portrayed in Christian iconography with a sword, did not hesitate to demonstrate to the "holder of the keys", his sharp rectitude.

The Roman Church boasted highly of the presence of the two apostles in Rome, venerating them from the very beginning as its co-founders, associating them in the cult and firmly joining their images in the official iconography.

The primeval church of St. Peter's already had sculptural figures of both apostles flanking the entrance staircase; the two 15th-century statues, substituted during the pontificate of Pope Pius IX (1846-78), by the statues now on view there, are presently displayed in the Biblioteca Latina of Nicholas V and Sixtus IV (in the vestibule of the Upper Hall).

The obelisk (or *guglia*, as it was referred to in the old plans and views) was the first actual feature of that large square. It was transported by Caligula from Egypt into his circus in the Vatican, to decorate the center, and there it remained until the end of the 16th century, near the sacristy, south of the basilica, where a stone marking that site is still found today. In 1586 the obelisk was transported to the center of the still unfinished square; this way a highly-acclaimed task of construction engineering, directed by Domenico Fontana. The year 1612 saw the arrival of the fountain designed by Carlo Maderno (on the right as one faces the church), as well as the controversial lengthening of the central nave and the completion of the façade. Finally, the work of Gian Lorenzo Bernini will materialize to tie everything together.

St. Peter's tomb has always been the heart of the church, both of the old and the new. It was on the site of this tomb that building began during the 2nd century, later demolished and replaced by new

6

7

4. *St. Peter's Square with faithful*

5. *Giuseppe de Fabris, Statue of St. Peter*

6. *Adamo Tadolini, Statue of St. Paul*

7. *Jean Paul II blessing the faithful in St. Peter's Square*

8. *St. Peter's Square and the Apostolic Palace*

9. St. Peter's Dome

building in the mid-15th century. The ostensible reason for this last undertaking was the decaying state of the edifice; the real reason for the alteration being the urgency to redesign both the church and the urban plan of the entire Vatican area. The undertaking may by considered a sanctioned response by Christian Rome to the sollicitations of the nascent humanist culture. It is precisely the humanism of Nicholas V, Leon Battista Alberti and Fra Angelico, and the spirit of the high Renaissance of Julius II, Bramante and Michelangelo which will express very clearly the new cultural synthesis. According to a statement attributed to Bramante, the theme of the projected reconstruction was: "to place the Pantheon over the vaults of the Temple of Peace" (that is, the old church). Though very spacious, the church's interior was architecturally unified; the classical exterior, its dome dominating the mausoleum, was a clear reflection of the tomb below. Bramante's original architectural concept was considered by Michelangelo (called by Paul III in 1547 to direct the construction of the building) as the "truth", the first stone being laid in 1506. Michelangelo cast invections against the "sangallesques", those supporters of Antonio da Sangallo, one of the first promoters of the plan to elongate the church. Sangallo's plan, as well as that followed by Maderno and Paul V, called for the addition of two ambulatory arcades to the central nave (an alteration made for liturgical purposes) and the consequent enlargement of the façade so that whoever today stands in front of the church will find it almost impossible to see the dome. Bernini's intervention may therefore be seen as all the more genious, for by means of the square he made the church a cohesive whole once again, and by means of the colonnade, dubbed the famous "embrace", reclaimed the

10. *The fountain on the right of Saint Peter's Square*

dome, the edifice's "mind". No paradox is intended when it is said that the dome and the monument's centrality more actively participate in the overall setting when one looks at the square from the church, rather than when one looks directly at the façade from the square.

Between 1657 and 1667 the colonnade was crowned by statues of saints, created by an array of sculptors under Bernini's guidance. That period also saw the arrival of the fountain on the left and the two covered corridors that were connected to the atrium of the building. Two hundred and eighty-four columns, each fifteen meters in height, and eighty-eight pilasters form the two "arms" of the square, (the metaphor is Bernini's who, with the controlled height of the colonnade and the slight converging of the two corridors, wanted to give a greater vertical lift to the façade, creating a rapport similar to that which exists between the arms and trunk of the human body, all culminating in the dome, its "head").

In the square, the many pilgrims and the many statues are part of the same scene and are actors in the same reality. The square could not better express its triumphant affirmation of centrality, a notion which was supported by the Roman Church following the Counter Reformation. The *itinerarium mentis* was announced by Bernini's angels on the St. Angelo Bridge, exhibitors of the instruments of Christ's Passion. The procession commenced on a low, sentimental note, just across the Tiber River. The cortège, in the original urban surroundings of the dense Vatican Borgo, was then taken by surprise more so than today by the sudden wide open space of the square. The advance of the procession is clearly indicated and coreographically driven along the three concentric corridors covered by the

11. The bell and the clock on the façade of the basilica

12. The apse of the basilica

13. View of the dome

14. View of the nave

colonnade. Through the irritating centrality of the *Burghesius* (Paul V's family name) which occupies the center of the façade's architrave, we are reminded of the mundane contradiction which that thrust drags along with it, with evidence that makes fun of the intentions of he who placed it there.

It has often been observed that when one stands in front of the immense deserted nave of the church, one finds oneself disconcerted rather than impressed. The parity of the dimensions (186 meters long, the main vault 44 meters high) mollifies every tension without creating any in either the horizontal or the vertical sense. The luminous lantern of the dome, being for too distant and thus imperceptible, leaves us without any point of reference. The eye searches the nearest pilasters and walls, which forecast the church's superabundant ornamentation; starting points for our itinerary.

And the response offered by the church's detail is ready: a pontiff's funeral monument in the lower part of the wall, the statue of a saint high up in the niches, or the measure of a famous cathedral, inscripted with bronze letters in the pavement. The visitor remains captivated by the detail, and it is difficult for the faithful not to wane into tourists. The temple decomposes into a constelled plan of numbers; the allurement of St. Peter's Tomb, knowingly orchestrated to this point, seems to have been almost dispersed. Yet, during the special moments of liturgical solemnity or during the exceptional liturgical events when the church fills up, the Pope and the faithful are present, the great

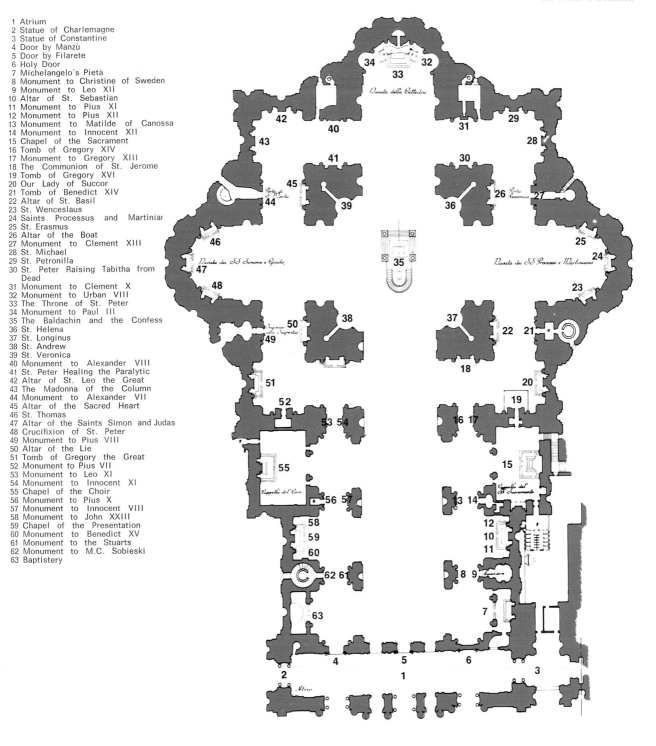

nave is once again unified and is full of life and sensation. The funeral monuments, the statues, the mosaics and the colossal inscriptions in the upper zone (which, in the empty church, even give Peter's evangelical steps an admonishing ring, a severe note reminiscent of the canons of the Council of Trent): all these express their own message in an apologetic chorus similar to a liturgical celebration, all regains a festive complementarity. Bernini's polychrome bronze invention, the baldachin, seems to become exactly what it always wanted to be: an almost mobile device wavering above a cult ceremony that is perennially being performed.

15,16. Michelangelo, the Pietà

When, in 1972, a madman mutilated and defaced Michelangelo's *Pietà*, the worldwide reaction served to establish the precise place that this work of art occupies in the history of our culture. It is not only a stronghold of the artistic world patrimony, but is also one of the most tender images that an artist's fantasy has presented to the faithful in the history of Christendom.

Before being transported in 1749 to its present location, the statue was placed in a *sacellum* of the Petronilla Chapel, founded by the actual commissioner, the French cardinal, Jean de Bilhères de Lagraulas, inside a *rotunda* (an ancient Roman mausoleum) attached to the southern transept of the old church.

Michelangelo arrived in Rome for the first time in 1496, already esteemed but not yet hallowed. Between 1498 and 1499, the twenty-four year old artist sculpted the Pietà. The amazement created by this work caused some critics to raise doubts about the true authorship of the Pietà; thus Michelangelo decided to sign his name on the Virgin's belt. One easily understands such doubts: this work has been defined as "pre-Bernini", i.e. more than a century ahead of its time. (A century during which Michelangelo hastened artistic development!)

17. *François Duquesnoy, Statue of St. Andrew*

18. *Francesco Mochi, Statue of Veronica*

19. *Gian Lorenzo Bernini, Monument of Alexander VII*

20. *Altar of Leo I the Great*

21. *Altar of Presentation*

22. *Baptistery Chapel*

23. *Antonio Canova, Monument of Clement XIII*

24. *Antonio Canova, Monument to the exiled Stuarts*

25. View of the nave from the dome   *26. Interior of the dome*

In order to understand Michelangelo's interpretation of the Pietà theme, one ought to consider another theme which he employed during these same early years: the Madonna and Child (recall the *Madonna of Bruges*). The Virgin, always looking faraway, detached from the young boy whom she nurses or who climbs on her knee; the serious look fixed in a project to which she clings, yet which is not hers. In the *Pietà*, on the other hand, the young boy is now the dead Redeemer and she, the Virgin, supports him and looks at him. The anguish that the elder Simeon foretold, expressed more by the hand than by the face, is now completely hers.

Michelangelo's frequent use of this theme, dear especially in the transalpine world in which the seeds of the Reformation were maturing, is recognized here in terms in which the same serene completeness indicates the perfect equilibrium between the described drama and the expressive potential of the artist's classical training. When, however, in the solitude of his later years, the artist confronts this theme once again (*Pietà in Florence*: 1547-55; *Rondanini Pietà*: 1552-64), the two figures embracing and almost falling down together are united in a common Passion. It is a simple and powerful synthesis that sweeps away the nascent polemics regarding the role of the Virgin in the Redemption, polemics born out of the confrontation between the scriptural (Gn. 3:15), embraced by Protestantism, and the tradition of the Vulgate, which the Council of Trent was preparing to declare canonical.

But regarding this new vision or artistic approach of his later years, technical accidents or personal dissatisfaction did not allow the artist to conclude his work with a perfect formal and polished mantle. Infact, it was more often he himself who, with the blows of a hammer, destroyed works destined to remain incomplete.

The decoration of the interior of the church establishes a true *summa* image of the Roman Church left by the Council of Trent. Around the great reliquary of St. Peter's Tomb are four pilasters supporting

27. *Gian Lorenzo Bernini, the Triumph of the Chair of St. Peter*

28. *The baldaquin and the altar of the Confession*

the dome; they are dedicated to other famous relics, which are also alluded to by the statues in the niches. Those relics are: the Lance of *S. Longino* (the anonymous Roman soldier who pierced Christ's side on Calvary), *Veronica*'s Cloth (the icon bearing the Holy Face of Christ), the Wood of the Cross (brought to Rome by *St. Helen*) and the Head of the apostle *Andrew*. Different in terms of history and the antiquity of the cult, the four personified relics attain, due to their enormous proportions and the emphasis of their baroque nature, an impetuous legitimation which could not be farther from the purists' spirit that the cult of the relics underwent from the very beginning of the Church (St. Jerome, *Adversus Vigilantium* 8).

A dictionary of erudition from the last century defines mosaic as: "a type of painting that is the most durable kind found; being such, its beauty endures in those locations where the work made with colors is consumed with the passage of time". This concept plus the illustrious Paleochristian tradition implied in the use of the art of mosaic soon associated itself to preoccupations about the deterioration of canvases which decorated various altars of the church and in which greater importance had been given to content than to pictorial quality. Thus, a special *studio del mosaico*, operating in the Vatican

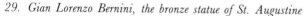

29. Gian Lorenzo Bernini, the bronze statue of St. Augustine

30. Arnolfo di Cambio (?), Statue of St. Peter

from the 16th century and institutionalised by Benedict XIII in 1727, slowly replaced with admirable, though cold reproductions, the original paintings on canvas.

Sculpture proves to be very much different, especially the papal funeral monuments. In these works of art each artist, from the late Renaissance to the present, while trying to capture the essence of each pontificate, at the same time brought to light specific characteristics of his art, almost to an emblematic point. So it was for the Bernini masterpieces dedicated to Urban VIII and Alexander VII, for Alessandro Algardi's sculpture of Leo XI, for Canova's Tomb of Clement XIII and his monument to the Exiled Stuarts.

The monument of Innocent VIII by Pollaiuolo was the only funeral monument moved from the old church into the new one. And this due to the sceneographic opening of that Tuscan "sepulchre in the air", accentuated by a rich bronze chromatism; its very originality in the combination of the images of the dead Pope asleep and the Pope alive and blessing, anticipated the hosanna-type inclination of monuments in the 17th century.

Two themes held dear by the early Christians and keypoints in the projected launching of the Counter Reformation were interpreted by Gian Lorenzo Bernini in an interesting and ingenious manner. The first theme was the authentic presence of St. Peter, the founder of the Roman Church, and the second theme, the primacy of his teaching. The first is marked by the baldachin placed over

31. The Niche of the Pallia, beneath the altar of the Confession

the Apostle's burial spot; the baldachin surges upwards, its twisted bronze colums re-echoing those once found in the presbytery of the old church. The second theme is expressed by the triumph of the Chair of Peter in the apse, supported by the Fathers of the Greek and Latin Church and illuminated by the Holy Spirit. The notion of the Chair of Peter, already alive in the 3rd century, was later firmly established in cult practice through the precious throne given to John VIII by Charles the Bald in 875. This throne, venerated as a relic of Peter, was solemnly placed in the reliquary seat conceived by Bernini on January 18, 1666.

With the transformation and the enlargement of the church the need was felt to become closer and more intimate with St. Peter's Tomb. Thus the primitive rapport between the church and its real center, its ideal center was upset. During the reign of Constantine the tomb was enveloped by a high marble monument clearly visible placed in the center of the transept. The raising of the presbytery towards the end of the 6th century, "so that Masses are celebrated over the Body of the Blessed Peter" (*Liber Pontificalis*), was extended throughout the entire church between the 16th and 17th centuries, thus making the floor of the ancient church into a crypt (the Grottoes) and the site of the tomb an underground point onto which the nave opens in the "Confession": an empty spot dimly lit, an intense pause in the full orchestration of the nave.

The Niche of the Pallia at the end of the open Confession and the Clementine Chapel at the

32. *Antonio del Pollaiolo, Monument of Sixtus IV. St. Peter's Treasure*

33. *Sarcophagus of Junius Bassus. St. Peter's Treasure*

enclosure of the Grottoes are the points in closest proximity to the Tomb. The first is nothing other than the enlarged version of the lower niche of the trophy that, since the 2nd century, has stood over the cavity containing the apostle's remains. Lambswool stoles, known as *pallia*, are conserved there in a silver reliquary. These *pallia* are annually woven and blessed, and "gathered from the body of Blessed Peter", and sent by the Pope as a symbol of the "plenitude of the pontifical office", to the newly-elected patriarchs and metropolitans.

The tourist finds a natural complement to his visit of the church in the Grottoes and in the Treasure of St. Peter's. The Grottoes house funeral monuments, remnants of the old church and also the archeological finds that came to light during the repeated excavations. The Treasure of St. Peter's, rearranged in 1974, consists of votive gifts, sacred ornaments and other reliquaries accumulated by St. Peter's during centuries of religious piety and prestige of the Roman Seat, a treasure which managed to survive various ancient and more recent pillages.

He who visits the church in the spirit of the ancient pilgrims will find that the stopping points which make up his itinerary are different, even if at times topographically similar. He will find the tombs of the last popes a few steps beyond the Apostolic Memorial in the Grottoes: those popes whom he knew, he saw and to whom he listened. He will see, finally, the successor in an audience, about which Pope Paul VI spoke using the words of St. Paul (Rom. 1:11-12) to inaugurate the new Hall (1971): "For I long to see you, that I may impart to you some spiritual gift to strengthen you, that is, that we may be mutually encouraged by each other's faith, both yours and mine".

34. *The Byzantine Cross of the emperor Justine II. St. Peter's Treasure*

35. *Byzantine Dalmatic. St. Peter's Treasures*

36. *The Audience Hall*

37. *Palace of Sixtus V, the present residence of the Pope*

THE PONTIFICAL PALACES

To the north of the church, high over the right arm of the colonnade, surge the edificies in which the Bishop of Rome permanently resides. Until the Middle Ages his natural abode was in the Lateran Patriarch's residence, beside which stood and still stands the Cathedral of Rome: St. John Lateran. Despite the obvious significance of the place, we find that the history of the popes' residence does not reflect "free choices", but rather the quest for the conditions of liberty. This phenomenon is evident from the beginning of the 6th century when Pope Simmaco (498-514), who was prohibited the use of the Lateran because of the Laurentian scism (and the unrest caused thereby), was the first to pass several years in the Vatican. There he constructed two *episcopia*, in truth modest enough, to the north and south of the church. Consider, too, that Leo IV (847-55) encircled the Vatican village with a wall; a place believed protected by its recognized sanctity, it was nevertheless pillaged during the Saracen invasions occurring during the pontificate of Sergio II (844-47). Innocent III (1198-1216) thought it useful that in Rome, bloodied by the violence of the factions, the Pope have a worthy abode "*eciam apud sanctum Petrum*". It was Nicholas III (1277-80) who enlarged the abode, thus establishing the first permanent residence and also setting down the indispensible premise for all future building developments. Finally, in this century it was Pius XI (1922-39) who saw in the legal capacity of the State, conferred by him on the leonine city (1929), a minimum guarantee of autonomy for his Ministry.

During the first centuries of the church, this was used by the Pope for overnight stops: during the liturgical celebrations, it allowed the Pope to present himself early in the morning. There edifices were equipped later to give hospitality to the Pope and his entourage; ultimately they became the palace, the medieval rock, the Renaissance royal palace, the seat of the modern sovereign, the autonomous contemporary state.

It is significant, given these events, to note the institution of the Swiss Guards, "*cohors pedestris*

38. *The bronze door*

39. *The Scala Regia*

40. *The Sala Regia, decorated by Giorgio Vasari*

Helvetiorum a sacra custodia Pontificis'', on January 21, 1506 when one hundred and fifty Swiss entered Rome through the Porta del Popolo, meeting at St. Peter's Square where Julius II blessed them, having agreed to their enlistment *''pro custodia palatii nostri''* with the Confederate States *''Superioris Alemanniae''*. This custody comprised of young German-speaking men from the Catholic Cantons, met the most rigorous and tragic test during the Sack of Rome (1527), when one hundred and forty-seven members fell in the atrium of the church. The Corps, which Marcello II wanted to dismiss in 1555, maintaining that the Pope had no need for armed defense, was many times dissolved and reinstituted; it grew and was reduced according to the political vicissitudes of the Roman Seat. In 1970, Paul VI dismissed the Armed Pontifical Corps, yet not the Swiss Guards; that is, he acquiesced to an ancient tradition (a proud and long-lived one) and to the marked symbolic quality which the Corps has assumed over a period of time.

42. Court of St. Damasus

41. View of the Loggias on the Court of St. Damasus   *43. John Paul II with the Swiss Gards in the Sala Ducale*

44. Pinturicchio, ceiling of the Room of the Saints

45. Pinturicchio, the Prophet Daniel and the Erythraean Sybil

46. Pinturicchio, the Resurrection

The first of the Pontifical Apartments found today in their original condition is that named after the family of Alexander VI (1492-1503), the Spaniard Rodrigo de Borja. It occupies part of the wing of Nicholas III's medieval palace (including the Pontiffs' Room destined for the solemn audiences), part of Nicholas V's wing (the Room of the Arts, the Saints and the Mysteries) and part of the northern tower, with which Alexander VI completed the projet of Nicholas V. Connected to the Arts Room which was used as a study, was a group of rooms in the western Niccolina wing; there the Pope had his private abode, and it was in the first of these rooms that he died on August 18, 1503.

It would be of little importance to summon up here the figure of that Pope, easily condemnable and quickly condemned. His bloody nature, in which intense piety and severity regarding doctrinal custody was combined with a cynical capacity for intrigue, worldly ambition, fast and unbridled sensuality mixed with incredible passion and violence; this personality of his seems to us a key to

understanding that test which he himself sollicited, calling, between 1492 and 1494, the Umbrian artists Bernardino di Betto Bardi, better known as Pinturicchio, and those under his guidance, Benedetto Bonfigli Perugino, Tiberio d'Assisi, Piermatteo d'Amelia, Pietro d'Andrea da Volterra and Antonio da Viterbo.

The traditional themes, the religious and humanistic iconography (from the *Annunciation* to the *Resurrection*, from *Arithmetic* to *Music*), the luminous Umbrian landscape, the elegant architecture, play host to exotic persons and magnificent costumes, almost overloaded with vibrant colours and blazing gilding. It would be difficult not to recognize the self-portrait of the commissioner, whom Pinturicchio seems to have understood in the portrait reproduced here, and the reality to which these rooms formed a back-cloth.

47. Pinturicchio, the Arithmetic

48. Raphael, the School of Athens

Julius II (1503-13) Alexander's successor (Pius III was actually his immediate predecessor although he served for little more than a month) resisted the intensity of this evocation for only four years. With the death of Cesare Borgia on March 12, 1507, the last and the most menacing cloud of the Borgian heredity was dissolved. On November 16, 1507, the Pope sought to solemnize the anniversary of his coronation by going to live on the upper floor of the same wing of Nicholas III and Nicholas V's palace because "he did not want to continually see the image of Alexander, his predecessor and enemy. . ." as his Master of Ceremonies Paride de Grassis recounts. This Pope was described by his contemporaries in these terms. Francis I, King of France, said to Leo X, Julius' immediate successor: "In this century we have never known a more formidable adversary than Pope Julius". The historian Raffaele Maffei da Volterra describes him as: "born to arms and to fulfil the role of army commander rather than to religion", and we have already seen him as the founder of the Swiss Guards. A Venetian ambassador, Girolamo Lippomano remarked upon "his terrible heart in everything"; and another, Domenico Trevisano averred that: "the Pope wanted to be the *dominus* (lord) and master of the world". Concern was shown by Ferdinand the Catholic of Spain who wrote to his own ambassador, Francisco de Rojas, that the Pope's intention was to make Rome "the center of the world". All of this plus a great personal austerity, acknowledged by the Florentine historian Francesco Guicciardini. From the first days of his Pontificate this awesome talent and energy was directed towards a very clear goal: the re-establishment and consolidation of the temporal dominion of the Church, conceived simply as an indispensable support of his mission. It is not surprising that this man saw every project regarding the Vatican, the center of such universal prestige, as an episode strictly geared to the illustration of historic, cultural and theological themes which would legitimize that design. Nor is it surprising that in order to realize such a "symbol come papal seat", he called upon the richest personalities of the High Renaissance: the architect Donato Bramante, the painter Raphael of Urbino and "Michelangelo, the sculptor" whom he compelled to paint frescoes. He

49. Raphael, the School of Athens, detail   *50. View of the Room of the Segnatura*

51. Raphael, the Dispute on the Blessed Sacrament

managed all of them as they handled the square rule, paintbrush or chisel, allowing them liberties at one moment, and at others forcing them unwillingly to his own ends.

The twenty-five year old Raphael, arriving in Rome in 1508, was immediately put to the test in the room later to be called the Stanza della Segnatura. Julius II soon commissioned him to fresco the entire Grand Apartment; in order to avoid incoherences in the language or deviations in the organic exposition of the themes which he, Julius, had chosen, he removed the paintings by Piero della Francesca, Luca Signorelli, Lorenzo Lotto, Sodoma and Peruzzi. Only the ceiling by Perugino in the Stanza dell'Incendio was spared, thanks to his pious student Raphael. (The themes were elaborated by a group of the most esteemed Humanists at court: Sigismondo de' Conti or Jacopo Sadoleto, Pietro Bembo or Baldassare Castiglione and by Neoplatonic philosophers of the school of Marsilius Ficino).

The Stanza della Segnatura was probably meant to be the Pope's private library and study; perhaps it was so named because it was there that the official acts and signing of documents took place. The program represented in the Stanza is that of Truth, Beauty and Goodness; these values, the highest obtainable within human experience, are enriched by Revelation, while human experience itself is in turn strengthened by Faith and Grace. It was a difficult theme for one who was no longer content to employ the elegant, singular allegories or personifications of Sciences, Virtues and Arts. Here every theme bears a double "realization". The first one consists in its translation into an episode, imaginary but concrete, an account where real protagonists of history are seen acting. The second realization is obtained by attributing portraits of contemporary men to historical figures included in the scene. A full and convincing measure is thus conferred on this story so that it is far from vexatious anachronism or abstract atemporality. The most mythical past is realized in one transparent history in which all human experience is contemporary.

52. Raphael, the Parnassus

The first fresco faced by Raphael is usually referred to as the *Dispute of the Holy Sacrament*. The militant Church is represented in the lower zone, the Church triumphant in the upper zone, and both are diachronically arranged: Gregory the Great, Ambrose and Dante contemplate the Mystery of the Eucharist, and Abraham, Peter and Lawrence are depicted contemplanting the vision of the Trinity. There is a very evident horizontal caesura of the field, crossed only by the hidden vertical that rises from the ostensory to the Holy Spirit, to the Son and the Father.

The *School of Athens* is Human Science. In a large hall, which echoes Bramante's project for the new St. Peter's, Raphael sees the sages of history, ancient as well as contemporary, gathered together and has arranged them according to their various disciplines. With Plato and Aristotle advancing in the center, the various groups signify a multi-natured, diversified and animated work. The daring placement of the statues of Apollo and Athena in the niches, like those of the saints in St. Peter's, is typically Neoplatonic.

The problem of the wall which is broken up by a window in both the ''autograph'' rooms, the Stanza della Segnatura and the Stanza of Heliodorus, was resolved by Raphael in four different ways. To the north, opening onto the Belvedere courtyard which rises towards Monte S. Egidio, there is the depiction of Parnassus. Apollo and the Muses, Homer and the ancient and modern poets, descending by the window, are explicitly linked to the scholars who frequented the Papal Library. (On the right, Pindar's gesture is clear). The fresco opposite Parnassus is the only one in which the actual window architecture has been incorporated and developed in the painted architecture. The marvelous figures of the *Cardinal Virtues* in the lunette, traditionally personified, reveal how much the Sybils of the Sistine Chapel vault (unveiled in August 1511) were present in Raphael's mind in their sobre chromaticism and robust forms (compare them to the Muses of *Parnassus*!) and in their relationship to the architecture.

53. Raphael, St. Peter delivered from prison   *54. Raphael, St. Peter delivered from prison, detail*

The theme of the Stanza of Heliodorus is simpler: faith in God in defense of His Church, heir to the people of the Old Testament, is evoked. We find here some of the most inspired pages which the Holy Scriptures have dictated to painting. Raphael reveals an extraordinary, youthful flexibility which enables him to use the theme of the text as a pretence for radical pictorial inventions. He will also do this in the later *Transfiguration*. The first fresco illustrates a passage from the second book of Maccabees (3:15-18), narrating the attempt by Heliodorus to confiscate the treasure of the Temple of Jerusalem at the behest of Seleucus IV of Syria (186-175 B.C.). Heliodorus was thwarted in this attempt by a "horse mounted by a terrible horseman" and by "two youths"; the heaven-sent reply from God to the prayers of the High Priest Onias. The *Mass of Bolsena* records the famous miracle of 1263 that occurred in the church of St. Christine in Bolsena when a Bohemian priest, suffering from doubts about the Transubstantiation, is confirmed in his faith when he sees blood miraculously issuing forth from the Host onto the corporal during the Consecration. On the north wall is the *Deliverance of St. Peter from Prison* (Acts 12:4-10). Light and night, passing references in the text, here become key elements in the pictorial representation; the homage to the Pope, once the titular cardinal of St. Peter in Chains; the assimilation of Venetian colour; yet another variation on the theme of the window: all combine together in a perfect invention. The marvelous left-hand group of the last painting, the *Meeting between St. Leo the Great and Attila*, is certainly by Raphael but the rest of the painting displays a certain reliance on the aid of his pupils and a certain heaviness in the *maniera*. This situation will repeat itself in the Stanza dell'Incendio and that of Constantine where Raphael did less and less of the actual painting. As he became less involved, there followed an impoverishment in the choice of themes which were treated in a more mannered fashion. This fresco contains both the figures of Julius II (between Leo IV and Attila) and Leo X, his successor, in cardinal's robes. Upon Julius II's death, his portrait was replaced by that of Leo X. A "unity of name" is established between the figures of the two Leos, IV and X and forms the tenuous link with the episodes of the third room. Little more

55. *Raphael's school, ceiling of the Room of Heliodorus*   56. *Raphael, the Miracle of Bolsena*

57. *Raphael, the Fire in the Borgo*

58. *The Pope's private study*

59. *The Pope's private chapel*

60. *St. Peter's Square with faithful from the Pope's window*

than a courtly *calembour* (play on words), not unpleasing to the Medici Pope, it was however too weak a pretext to capture Raphael's imagination.

To conclude our survey of the most famous of the stanze and before examining the oratories and chapels of the palace, we would like to look at some of the areas and places where the Pope spends his days. This section does not intend to draw comparisons but to remind and point out that these monuments should be seen in the light of their functions which are still valid.

61. Fra Angelico, St. Sixtus ordains St. Lawrence

In March of 1455, Nicholas V (1447-55) and the Dominican painter Fra Giovanni da Fiesole (1387-1455), better known as Fra Angelico, died within one week of each other. Of the paintings by Fra Angelico commissioned by Nicholas V, only those in the *Chapel of Nicholas V* remain intact. The theme employed there of the parallel stories of the deacons Stephen and Lawrence, from their mission to their martyrdom, was apparently held dear by the Pope because effigies of these two saints appeared in the stained glass windows of the Pope's study. The devote, learned and humble Pope (who liked to recall his origins as "a priest who rings the bells") had such a brief pontificate that he was only able to begin the vast building project he had in mind: the reconstruction of St. Peter's, the enlargement of the palace and its enclosure within the mighty bastions and finally, the remodelling of the entire Vatican Borgo. But the spirit of this peaceful interpreter of the greatness of the Church, which he intended to advance with "only the arms . . . that Christ gave me for my defense, that is, His Cross", is reflected perfectly in this simple oratory, the work of that celestial painter, whom Vasari quoted as saying: "whoever wishes to depict Christ must always be with Christ".

62. View of the Chapel of Nicholas V

63. Sistine Chapel

64. Reconstruction of the original decorative program of the Sistine Chapel before Michelangelo's frescoes

Sixtus IV (1471-84) followed Nicholas in two of his undertakings: "books and building". In fact, he founded the Vatican Library and reconstructed the Capella Magna (the Sistine Chapel) of Nicholas III's palace, while simultaneously making in the angular bastion of the southwest section of the fort which had been enlarged by Pope Parentucelli. The simple plan of the Sistine Chapel repeats the measurements of the Temple of Solomon; 60 cubits by 20 cubits (Kings 6:2), equivalent to 40.23 meters by 13.41 meters, 20.70 meters in height. The correlation of these measurements anticipate the parallel stories of Christ and Moses which were to be depicted on the walls. The area above the vaults could accomodate a garrison ready for action and the openings between the corbels, at the topmost part of the exterior, speak of shots and boiling oil . . . Let us recall the words of Ludwig von Pastor: "This building served two purposes: the celebration of liturgical functions and the defense of the Vatican. It is a true symbol of that curious time when the beaux arts flourished in Italy amidst the clamour of arms. Only too often did the popes lay aside their mitre and cope, girding themselves instead with armour and replacing the mitre with a helmet". The project, probably by Baccio Pontelli, was executed by Giovannino de' Dolci (1475) and called for the complete pictorial decoration of the interior. On the large vault with lunettes, a simple blue ceiling with gold-coloured wooden stars was forseen; the first thirty-one popes of the Church were to be depicted in the upper zone between the windows; below, two fresco cycles with eight paintings in each, illustrating episodes from the life of Christ on one side, and those from that of Moses on the other. Over the altar a fresco depicted the Assumption of the Virgin, to whom the chapel was dedicated. Tapestries were painted around the base of the walls and these were to be covered by real tapestries on solemn occasions. Three paintings on the far wall where to be replaced by Michelangelo's *Last Judgment*; the two above the entrance perished during the time of Hadrian VI (1522-23). The paintings were executed between 1481 and 1483 by the Tuscan artists Botticelli, Ghirlandaio, Rosselli and Signorelli and by the Umbrians Perugino and Pinturicchio. The intentional parallelism of the episodes chosen from the Old and New Testaments seems to be confirmed by the fact that at least four of the original eight pairs of frescoes

65. *Interior of the Sistine Chapel*

66. *Perugino, the Giving of the Keys to St. Peter*

67. *Sandro Botticelli, the Punishment of Korah, Datan and Abiron*

51

68. Domenico Ghirlandaio, the Calling of the Apostles

69. Luca Signorelli, Moses gives his staff to Joshua and Death of Moses

were entrusted to the same hand—or school. The first pair of frescoes (*Birth of Christ* and the *Finding of Moses*—now lost) were by Perugino as well as the second pair (the *Baptism of Christ* and the *Circumcision of Moses*—the latter possibly by Pinturicchio); the third pair (the *Temptation of Christ* and the *Vocation of Moses*) were painted by Botticelli and the fifth pair (the *Law of Sinai* and the *Sermon on the Mount*) by Cosimo Rosselli. This balanced schema is broken by the fourth pair of frescoes in which the *Crossing of the Red Sea*, by Rosselli, corresponds to the *Calling of the Apostles* by Ghirlandaio and again in the penultimate pair where the *Last Supper* is linked to the *Testament of Moses* by Signorelli who was also responsible for the *Dispute over the Body of Moses* (now lost), corresponding with the *Resurrection* by Ghirlandaio in the last pair. In addition to the undisputed conceptual coherence of contrasting themes (although these are interpreted in various ways), references to contemporary events are present, supported by the portraits of actual personnages and by the self-portraits of the artists themselves. The sixth pair of paintings (actually, the fifth extant), Botticelli's *Punishment of Korah, Datan and Abiron* and Perugino's *Giving of the Keys to St. Peter*, constitutes a warning to the opponents of the Primacy of Peter in the parallel drawn by the divine punishment of the rebels in the Old Testament story. This link seems to be reinforced by the exchange of the background of the two episodes: Rome and its monuments for Moses and the Temple of Solomon for Christ and Peter. In that moment, this programme must have recalled the Andrea Zamometic affair. Zamometic was a Dominican Bishop from Grannea who instigated a council in violent contrast with the Pope in the Basle cathedral in March of 1482. One usually recognizes this same Zamometic in the figure on the right of Botticelli's fresco wearing the garb of a man soon to be stoned. As regards the Miracle of the Red Sea closing upon the Egyptians, it was not difficult for this work to recall, at that time, the expulsion of the Turks from Italy in 1481 when Sixtus IV was forced to call a crusade.

In February of 1508 Michelangelo saw his colossal bronze statue of Julius II unveiled in St. Petronius in Bologna. When he was initially entrusted with this commission, Michelangelo claimed to be inexperienced in bronze casting. After less than a month had passed, an even more extraordinary

70. *Michelangelo, the ceiling frescoes*

71. *Michelangelo, the Creation of the Planets*

72. *Michelangelo, the Creation of Adam*

assignment, which would force him to lay aside his chisel once again and which he at first clearly refused to undertake, was forced upon him by the Pope. This assignment was to paint, and what is more in fresco, the twelve apostles on the corbels of the lunettes under the vault of the Sistine Chapel. It was a useless refusal. Michelangelo began working in May and by the summer, even though he had accepted this commission so unwillingly, the work was growing in his hands so that he told the Pope that the painting of the twelve apostles was a ''meagre thing'' and that he wished to be given a free hand. In his celebrated sonnet to Vittoria Colonna, Michelangelo considered his creative process as a sculptor who sees a pre-existing figure in the depths of the marble which is waiting in expectation of the ''hand that obeys the intellect''. Indeed, it is impossible not to relate this aspect to Michelangelo the painter who, working modestly in a marginal area of that great vault, gradually saw it fill with figures. He was to respond to their appeal, even at the cost of having to cancel some of his works which he had already completed.

73. Michelangelo, the Fall and the Expulsion from Eden   74. Michelangelo, the Flood, detail

In this way the imposing painted scaffolding of the vault came to life: with space, depth and volume available for that painter who considered himself a sculptor exiled among the paintbrushes. The architraves crisscrossing the vault stand out for they do not accord with the pilasters between the windows, as would be expected. Thus they create an illusion of depth which would be occupied by the figures of the Phophets and Sybils. The sky opens up above the scaffolding to receive the scenes from the Creation. It seems that Michelangelo was not totally unaware of the Roman paintings of the II and III style which were then being discovered in that dawn of archeological research. Proceeding from the far wall we find *God Dividing Light from Darkness*, the *Creation of the Sun and the Moon* and the *Creation of the Plants*, *God Dividing the Waters and the Earth*, the *Creation of Man* (Adam), the *Creation of Woman* (Eve), the *Fall of Man* and the *Expulsion from the Garden of Eden*, *Noah's Offering*, the *Great Flood* and *Noah's Drunkness* in five major and four minor episodes. Recognizing his own inexperience in the fresco medium, Michelangelo wished to start from the last episodes. In fact, in the first one painted, the Flood, the multitude of small figures tends to obscure the carefully reasoned composition. It would be an error, though, to consider this progressive simplification of the scenes and the gradual enlargement of the figures as involuntary. Going back from the articulated drama of evil and innocence, the saved and the lost, to the simplicity of the rapport between the Creator and our progenitors, one finally reaches the superb solitude of His Presence, of His will, expressed without words by a look alone. In this first episode the boldness of the veristic vision embues with meaning the evanescence of the apparition of the Deity. It is pointless to add to the torrent of words already written about these images. It is sufficient to recognize the extraordinary complexity of the style which serves this acute and original interpretation; one example of this would be the transformation of the figure of the Creator, almost a visible "translation" of the concept of the "First Motor" or "First Cause", in the frescoes of the first days of Creation. He then becomes a massive, solemn and rock-like figure—a venerable Father—before Adam and Eve. Contrary to Biblical sources, God is absent from the scenes of the Fall of Man and the Expulsion; this is most certainly not an involuntary omission because the whole cycle deals with the theme of the non-presence of the "Hidden God", to be reclaimed by the Redemption. The *Prophets*, *Sybils*, *Nude Youths* repeat the plasticity and limpid design of the figure of Adam and convey the "absolute" humanity in a specific tension of thought, sentiment and vision. Instead, the *Ancestors of Christ* are immersed in the brownish tones found in the projections and the lunettes, as if they were waiting in dimly lit anonymity to receive light and form from the One who will come.

75. *Michelangelo, the Prophet Joel*

76. Michelangelo, the Delphic Sibyl (after the recent cleaning)

77. Michelangelo, Nude

78. *Michelangelo, Nude (after the recent cleaning)*

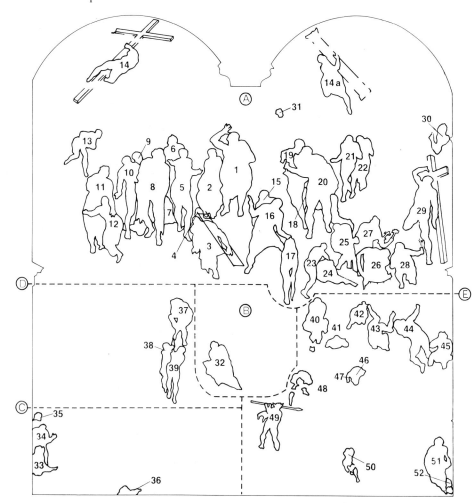

A Celestial World
1 Christ the Judge
2 Madonna
3 St. Lawrence
4 St. Martha, or St. Anne, Vittoria Colonna
5 St. Andrew, or the Baptist, Dismas
6 Rachel or Beatrice
7 Noah, or Enoch, or Paul III
8 St. John the Baptist, or Adam
9 Abraham, or St. Bernard, Pope Julius II
10 Abel, or Eve
11, 12 Niobe and daughter, or Eve and daughter, personification of motherhood, the merciful Church and a Christian
13 Pharaoh's daughter who found Moses, or Sarah, or Eve
14 Archangel Gabriel
15 Francesco Amadori of Urbino, or Tommaso de' Cavalieri
16 St. Bartholomew
17 St. Bartholomew's skin on which is depicted a portrait of Michelangelo
18 St. Mark, or Pope Clement VII
19 St. Paul
20 St. Peter
21 Job, or Adam, or Abraham
22 The Wife of Job, or Eve, Pope Hadrian VI
23 St. Longinus
24 Simon Zelotes
25 St. Philip or Dismas
26 St. Catherine of Alexandria
27 St. Blaise
28 St. Sebastian
29 Dismas, or St. Francis of Assisi, St. Andrew, Simon of Cyrene, the incarnation of Justice, the symbol of man and his afflictions
30 Moses or Adam
31 The wife of Salomon, or Dante Alighieri

B Trumpeting Angels
32 Archangel Michael with the book of the Elect

C Resurrection of the Dead
33 Dante
34 Michelangelo, or Pope Julius II, Virgil, St. Stephen, Plato (or Wisdom), the rescuer monk, an angel, Martin Luther
35 Michelangelo
36 Savonarola

D The Judged Ascending to Heaven
37, 38, 39 One of the Blessed (or an angel) supporting two negroes

E The Damned Hurled down towards Hell
40 One of the proud, or one of the damned for disperation (in contrast with theological hope)
41 A devil
42 One of the proud, or one of the lazy
43 One of the avaricious, or one of the simoniac popes, Nicholas III
44 One of the angry, or one of the proud
45 One of the lustful seized by a devil
46, 47 Paolo and Francesca
48 One of the proud, or one of the fraudulent
49 Charon or Satan made to ressemble the Bourbon constable
50 Cesare Borgia
51 Minos made to ressemble Biagio da Cesena
52, 53 Count Ugolino and the Archbishop Ruggeri

Thank to a recent cleaning, during which the layers of grime and lampblack that had settled on the wall surface over the centuries were removed, we can now admire this extraordinary frescoe cycle in all the splendour of its original colours.

Giulio de' Medici became Pope in 1523 and his pontificate, under the name of Clement VII, lasted until 1534. The most pointed example of this Pope's ''Medicean'' aspirations and the terrible times of his reign, is to be found in the commission which he entrusted to Michelangelo only a few months before his death: the painting of a ''Resurrection'' on the far wall of the Sistine Chapel. In May 1527 Rome had been subjected to the horrors of the Sack: murder, theft, devastation, all types of violence were not spared her. While the Pope was held prisoner in Castel Sant'Angelo his Vatican dwelling was taken over by Filiberto d'Orange and the Sistine Chapel was used as a stable. There were many who interpreted this catastrophy as God's vendication for the corruption which had been rampant in Rome. Among them was Clement VII himself, who wished the theme of the Last Judgment to be included in his principal chapel, and wished it to dominate the altar wall, rather than the entrance, contrary to medieval practice. It was meant as a constant reminder of the ineluctability of Divine Justice. Michelangelo began the work in the spring of 1536, completing it in 1541. It was Paul III who saw it finished.

79. Michelangelo, the Last Judgement

Of all of Michelangelo's works, the Last Judgment is the one which was most observed, awaited, copied, exalted and condemned. He himself forecast this: "how many will this work of mine drive mad!". It was a radical departure from accepted canons. Centred around the Herculean and Apollonian figure of Christ—too Herculean and too Apollonian the critics would say—figures abound, as if caught up in a whirlwind. The paintings by Perugino and Michelangelo himself, which had been on this wall, were cancelled so that the wall could disappear as a concrete entity and become a ground for an authentic vision, going beyond the bounds of the architecture itself. We find the figures from the Resurrection of the Dead in the lower left, the Ascent of the Blessed into Paradise, where angels

80. Michelangelo, the Last Judgement, detail of Christ

81. The mobile scaffolding used for cleaning the ceiling frescoes

carry the instruments of Christ's Passion; on the right the Fall of the Damned towards Hell, where they gather around Charon's boat. The figure of Christ is surrounded by a smaller circle with the figures of several saints and the Virgin: these share, one would say, more the anguish of the judged than the steadfastness of the Judge; as Tommaso da Celano said in his celebrated *Dies irae: "cum vix justus sit securus"*. Tommaso da Celano's writings as well as Dante's *Divine Comedy*, the Scriptures and the figurative depiction of the divine and the demonic elaborated by the pagan culture served as inspiration for Michelangelo.

82. *Michelangelo, the Conversion of Saul*

Between 1542 and 1549 Michelangelo worked as a painter for the last time in this chapel designed by
Antonio da Sangallo the Younger. Then in his seventies, Michelangelo was completing the funeral
monument for Julius II (more modest than first envisioned) with the statue of Moses (1545). He also
agreed to direct the reconstruction of St. Peter's in 1547. There were the usual resistance, the usual
results and the usual conditions: unlimited dedication and unlimited liberty; all admist the foreseen
envy, loneliness and incomprehension.
The first painting is the *Conversion of Saul*; the second is not the "symmetrical" Giving of the Keys

83. Michelangelo, the Crucifixion of St. Peter

but the *Crucifixion of St. Peter*. The same background as that in God's gesture in the Genesis scene—putrid green with blue-back mountains in the distance—the illusionistic space is fused to the real space by the figures only partially visible emerging from the lower part of the painting. A luminous diagonal descends from God's hand to Paul's face, and from him explode a series of oblique lines of movement. Opposite, admist the circular movement of figures who advance and retreat, is the gigantic figure of Peter whose stern face is directed towards the bystanders with the intensity and the audacity of one of St. Catherine of Siena's invectives.

84. Raphael's Loggia

86. Raphael's school, the Building of the ark

85. The Loggia decorated by Giovanni da Udine

87. Raphael's school, Moses found in the Nile

In June 1519, one of the most representative personalities of the Italian Renaissance, Baldassare Castiglione, wrote to Isabella d'Este: "Our Signore is more than ever involved in Music . . . he delights still in Architecture . . . and has provided himself with a painted loggia with stucco decoration in the antique manner, the work of Raphael, as beautiful as can be and perhaps more beautiful than the works one sees today". A few months later the Venetian Marcantonio Michiel, noted that "the Pope placed many statues there, . . . some had already been acquired by Pope Julius perhaps for that purpose, and were placed alternately in the hollow niches in the wall across from the columns and the pilasters . . .".

This is the Raphael Loggia, the second of the three superimposed loggias which, according to Bramante's plan elaborated and finished on his death (1514) by Raphael himself, scan the view towards the east of the medieval papal palace, on the present St. Damasus courtyard. There are thirteen decorated bays, stuccoed walls with grottesque figures after the manner of the ancients and a ceiling illustrating scenes from the Old and New Testaments. The ornamentation, executed by Raphael's students and assistants under the guide of their Master, is a blend of the sacred and the profane: but located as it is in a place free from religious significance it changes its accent, so to speak. If the *Belvedere Apollo* has been a source of inspiration for the Christ of the Sistine Chapel, the biblical scenes can dwell here beside the satyrs, sphinxes, nymphs and harpies, providing a pretext for

88. Raphael's school, the Donation of Rome

the light-hearted decoration of a place described by Michiel as being: "only for the pleasure of the Pope".

Leo X told Sebastiano del Piombo, the Venetian artist supported by Michelangelo, "In all honesty, I do not like the things they are making". He was referring to the work by Raphael's assistants who were decorating the fourth and most important of the official rooms of the Papal apartments (the Room of Constantine) after Raphael's death. They claimed to have his designs in hand but if their work did not meet with the approval of the Pope, he intended to "remove what they had done" and give the commission to Sebastiano del Piombo. With the help of Michelangelo, this artist promised to work miracles; actually it is clear that Leo sought to have Michelangelo himself work on this room "but he is terrible, as you see, one cannot have dealings with him". Unfortunately, Leo X died in 1521 and was succeeded by Hadrian VI whose little interest in this project drove those involved to near starvation. Under Clement VII's pontificate the work was completed by Giulio Romano and Penni in 1524.

89. Gallery of Maps

It was agreed that the themes were well chosen: the *Vision of Constantine, Constantine's Victory over Maxentius at the Milvian Bridge*, the *Baptism of Constantine* and his *Donation of Rome to Pope Sylvester*. However the quality of the paintings—decorative imitations of tapestries and stylistically reminiscent of Raphael—is almost a definition of the nascent phenomenon of ''Mannerism''. One can almost watch the birth of Mannerism in the bitter exclusion of talented artists and in the selection of Raphael's pupils as such, who were ready to extend their master's shadow to places it did not reach. High Mannerism, whose *trompe l'oeil* architecture, painting and perspective prepared the ground for the flowering of the Baroque, found in the scientific interests (particularly geography) of Gregory XIII an ideal source of pictorial suggestions where talent could be well exploited without being pushed beyond limits. One of the most balanced and successful *milieux* of the palace is the Gallery of Geographic Maps where the science of the Dominican Ignazio Danti (one of the ''genii'' in Gregory's staff for the Calendar Reform) was made *jucunda* by the art of Cesare Nebbia and a group of other painters within the architectural setting by Ottaviano Mascherino. The Pope however preferred the Quirinal Hill to that palace. Sixtus V (1585-90) also considered the Vatican residence to be unhealthy

90. *Jan Matejko, John Sobieski liberates Vienna, detail*   91. *The Sistine Hall of the Vatican Library*

and insufficient. The story of the Papal Palaces took a decisive turn during the last decades of the 16th century. Three palaces, all the work of Domenico Fontana, were built: one on the Quirinal (now the seat of the Head of the Italian State), one at the Lateran (the true seat of the Bishop of Rome, placed beside the cathedral) and one at the Vatican (where the Pope now resides, at the east of the previously existing buildings). The evolution of the buildings which developed from the medieval nucleus was arrested and an historically "aware" interpretation of them took over, making of them "shrines for art treasures", both memorable und untouchable. This process was completed over the years when the northern areas were destined for museum use where Julius II's Statue Garden, in the palace of Innocent VIII, will call for new developments and where both Sixtus V and Fontana found room to build the new Library.

THE VATICAN MUSEUMS

Leo X, who decorated Raphael's Loggia with antique sculptures, granting the 1551 edition of Tacitus by Beroaldo with his privilege, declared that he considered literature and the beaux arts to be among the greatest of his duties, God having given man nothing more useful than arts and letters except the knowledge and the true cult of His own divinity. Eighty years later, Sixtus V would order that the squares in front of the patriarchal basilicas be embellished with obelisks which had been carried away from Egypt by the Roman emperors. Just as he would crown the columns of Trajan and Marcus Aurelius with the statues of Peter and Paul, so he would place a cross on top of the obelisks, thus dedicating, as one of his biographers explains, "to the sign of salvation of human kind the monuments that antiquity, ignorant of the Truth, had dedicated to its fabulous gods". Where the crosses of the martyrs had been hoisted up, now "the same monuments of profanity submit to the

92. *Entrance to the Pio-Clementine Museum*　　　　　　93. *The Greek Cross Room of the Pio-Clementine Museum*

Cross and are transformed into the Cross''. Between the optimistic acceptance of antiquity of the former and the inquisitorial exorcism of the same by the latter stand the Reformation and Counter-Reformation. However, common to both is a monolithic vision of history, to be praised or condemned as if it were an individual life; as a positive or negative witness of an identical and eternal truth which envelops and dominates it all. The interpretation of the museums that have risen near the Apostolic Palace since the Renaissance (and up to the present day) oscillates between these two poles, in fact it includes both of them. Here we find the idea of the history of salvation as a real history, which can encompass the ancient and modern histories. This idea is the filtre through which all these treasures were seen and the scientific studies which have gradually developed more refined tools in order to read ancient civilizations more factually, have not been able to change their absolute location within that history.

The evolution of that motive which induced Sixtus V to exorcise the Egyptian obelisks is well expressed by the Barnabite Luigi Ungarelli, one of the first Italian Orientalists to interpret hieroglyphs according to Champollion's methods. Commenting on the Constitution of the Egyptian Museum (1839), Ungarelli, who was responsible for its arrangement, said: "It is fitting that Egyptian archeology, rather than remaining extraneous to the cause of religion, should ally itself with the latter''. And he continues: "Here theology recognizes the vestiges of the primitive traditions which preceded the written revelation of Moses and the prophets. Here . . . the sacred philology receives light for the better understanding of oriental biblical texts: how many points of contact comparative to the customs of the two populaces, the people of God and the Egyptians!''. The new museum contained materials of the old Capitoline fund from the Orti Sallustiani, from the Isaeum in Rome's Campus Martius and from the Canopus in Hadrian's Villa, and also the acquisitions made by the popes between the mid-18th century and the beginning of the 19th century. The "Egyptianizing"

94. *View of a room of the Egyptian Museum*

95. *Mask of a mummy*

96. *Gold hawk*

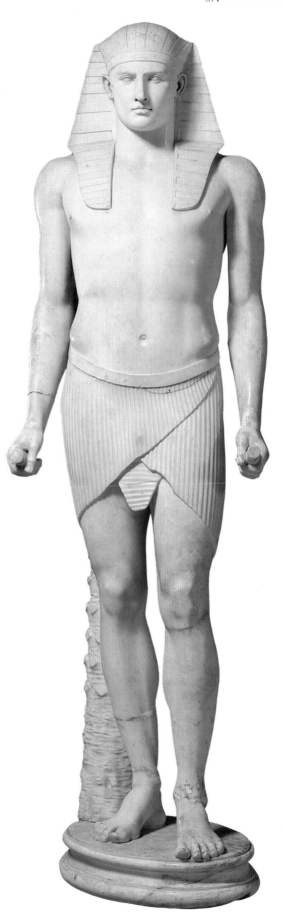

97. *Statue of Antinous*

98. View of the Regolini-Galassi Room

arrangement, although fanciful, did not intend to concede to that romantic approach, which in those days made Egyptology "admired more for the ignorance in which we were about it than for the little we knew of it", on the contrary the intention was to present the information according to "how much was needed for the constitution of a science".

The Gregorian Etruscan Museum, born two years earlier (2nd February, 1837) was much freer from similar ideological assumptions. Firstly because it was born out of lay needs, both administrative and scientific. This museum may be seen as the Pontifical State's answer to the problems posed by the unexpected explosion in archeological research in territory under its jurisdiction. This chaotic fervor for Etruscology, born out of the ashes of 17th century "Etruscheria", caused various problems, ranging from the control or direction of the archeological excavations to the selection and acquisition of finds, their restoration and exhibition. Secondly because the civilization on which these finds were throwing new light was soon to be labelled after "italic originality" its anti-classic tendencies, its unorthodoxy: features sufficient to protect if from the type of interpretations in which a cultural habit, now centuries old, had wrapped both Greek and Roman antiquity. Thus the habitual interpretations were impracticable when considering this new museum. Emphasis was therefore laid on such aspects as the considerable wealth of the finds, their technical finesse, the sign of a superior, refined and powerful civilization; also stressed was the originality of the figurative scenes with the language handed down through the inscriptions. All these are, of course, typically romantic considerations, all fed by the very unexpected and surprising nature of the re-emergence, in Tuscany and Latium, of the witnesses of that civilization. Though the exportation of first-rate archeological finds by these criteria and Etruscan collections have thus grown in many European cities. Nevertheless, the approach described above succeeded in gathering a highly significant collection. Between 1836-37, the wonderfully rich and almost intact Regolini-Galassi tomb was discovered in the necropolis of Cerveteri. This was considered such an important find that the Advisory Commission for Antiquity and Beaux Arts suggested to the Pontifical Government that they acquire it in its entirety. From the beginning of the study of this tomb, there was a strong suggestion of oriental influence; these links

99. Mars of Todi

100. Gold fibula from the Regolini-Galassi tomb

101. Female bust in terracotta

102. Funeral monument with Dying Adonis

103. View of the Court of the Pigna

were called upon to endorse the well-known theory concerning the eastern origins of the Etruscan people. This tomb is one of the most complete documents of the period of Etruscan civilization which lasted from the end of the 8th century to the early 6th century B.C.: a period referred to as "orientalising", which brought Etruria and more particularly the metropolis of Cerveteri into closer commercial and cultural contact with the principal Mediterranean centers. The so-called *Mars of Todi*, discovered in 1835, was immediately considered as representative of the technical evolution for which the Etruscans, particularly in their bronze work, were already esteemed among their contemporaries. This discovery also set off the first debates regarding the influence that classical Greek art had had on Etruscan art. Also housed here are hundreds of *ex-voto* terracottas which the Arch Priest of Cerveteri unearthed from his vineyard, on the site of the ancient Caere, in the early 19th century. There are entire statues, fragments of statues, particularly busts and heads; a wide range of works, varying in value and artistic quality, through which we are able to trace the development of the Etruscan portrait tradition to its maturity. Their witness added to that given by the archaic (canopic) cinerary urns and the later hellenistic urns from northern Etruria (particularly Chiusi) contribute to the starting of the secular dispute on the originality of portrait, as a figurative type, in the Etruscan ambience.

As we have seen, documents indigenous to the figurative Etruscan culture (tufa sculpture, terracotta, bronzes, jewellery) found their way into the new museum, being tentatively arranged at times according to the material used or the class to which these objects belonged, at others according to naïve attempts at reconstructions (a wall *panoplia*, a funeral chamber etc.). In evaluating Greek pottery, on the contrary, the culture and the taste of the time, found themselves much more at ease. It has been precisely the analysis of the numerous vases discovered during the first decades of the 19th century in the Etruscan city of Vulci (the city that provided nearly all the vases in the Gregorian collection) that, but a few years before the museum's opening, had definitely solved the problem of their place. Because of the high quality of the workmanship and the intelligibility of the themes depicted, these objects very soon became among the most deeply studied works of ancient art. Being particularly apt for interpretations and attribution, Greek pottery has had to pay a very high peculiar price. That is, while it has been used almost as a fossil-guide for the dating of archeological finds, it has often been isolated from its own historical and archeological context. This isolation still appears today in the main Etruscan museum.

"Not one of the vases that we have found so far could contend with this one for the palm given to the most finely executed work", said Antonio Nibby in 1834, presenting Exekias' famous amphora, donated to Gregory XVI by the Candelori brothers.

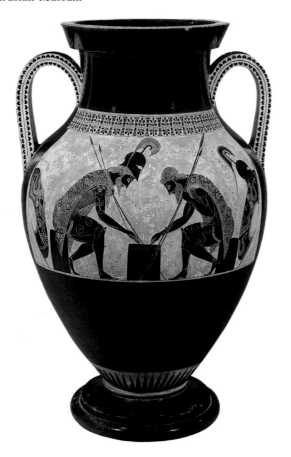

104. Amphora of Exekias　　　　　　　　　　　*105. Hydria of the Painter of Berlin*

This amphora came to Etruria from the Athenian workshop conducted by Exekias, the greatest potter working around 530 B.C. in the ceramic workers' quarter. During those years the old aristocratic class was subdued by the tyrant Peisistratos and this allowed small and medium entrepreneurs and traders to strengthen, supplanting on the Mediterranean coast, and particularly in Etruria, the Greek centers of Asia Minor and Peloponnesus.

Depicted on the principal side of this vase are Achilles and Ajax who, having cast aside their arms, play "morra"; and on the other side, Kyllaros, the horse tamed by Kastor, dominates the scene. Behind is Kastor, welcomed by Leda and Tyndaros and his brother Pollux. The black-figure technique was carried by Exekias to its extreme possibilities; surrounding his firmly composed, neat and exquisitely drawn figures with an empty space, the artist creates an intense contrast. Thus a feeling of depth and space, which the technical limitations would have levelled to two dimensions alone, is caused by the very tension which links the monumentality of the heroes. Peisistratos instituted, according to tradition in 534 B.C., the first tragic contests. If we had some record of Greek tragedy from Thespis' period to Phrynikos' (Aeschylus was born during this period), we would know what words to lend to these heroes. The hydria (a vase used to hold water) on which Apollo is depicted returning to Attica from the land of the Hyperboreans on his delphic tripod, dates between the period of Kleisthenes' democratic reforms and the Persian War (circa 490 B.C.). The "painter of Berlin", so-called after an amphora in Berlin that ranks among his major works, painted this vase, described by its 19th century discoverers as "first-rate, of exquisite beauty". The vase reflects the artist's taste, in keeping with the new humanism of this epoch. On the front, a sole figure—a self-sufficient world in itself—is superimposed on a compact and bright background; the pure design is enriched by a variety of tones made possible by the red-figure tecnique. Lightness and autonomy will from now on become peculiar features in the Greek depiction of Apollo: we shall meet them again, though differently developed, in the *Belvedere Apollo* and the *Apollo Souroktonos*.

106. View of the Octagonal Court

A recent interventions "purified" the Etruscan Museum, separating from its collection the Roman Antiquities with which they were previously interspersed. Greek sculptures that had been interwoven into the various galleries of the sculpture museums underwent a similar treatment. The scientific rigour of these operations, could not be farther from those cultural attitudes of the early 16th century which are accredited with the parentage of the Vatican's ancient sculpture collection. We have seen that during the early 16th century there was a vital integration of ancient classical works with the art and the culture of the time. In the already cited edition of Tacitus by Filippo Beroaldo, Leo X affirms that the study of antiquity is "of help in the most varied of circumstances: salutary during times of adversity, useful and decorous in favourable circumstances, so that without it every human care seems to lose its sense and every pleasure to be gained in civil company seems unable to exist in any fashion".

It is easy to imagine just how little space such an opinion leaves for impartial classification and historical appraisal. All cultures strongly inspired by a precise vision of man and his history refute the neutrality of a purely historicist contemplation of history: revolutions knock down monuments, they change the names of streets, squares and calendar months. There was a radical opposition to a purely learned collectionism and this is clearly indicated by the experience which the collection of antiquities before our eyes has undergone. Let us recall some of these events.

In 1503 the newly-elected Pope, Julius II, placed a statue of *Apollo* in the internal courtyard of the Belvedere Palace built by Innocent VIII, which had been transformed into a garden for the occasion. This was the same statue that Julius II had when he was a cardinal; it was then located in the garden of his titular church of St. Peter in Chains. Thus, the Vatican Museum was born. In 1506 the *Laocoön* was added to the collection, after its discovery on the Esquiline Hill before the eyes of Giuliano di Sangallo and Michelangelo. In 1566, Pope Pius V spoke of the unseemliness of "St. Peter's successor who would have such idols in his house". It was only following various

107. *Cabinet of Masks*   108. *Gallery of Statues*

remonstrances by the Curia that Pius V accepted that the statues remain where they were because of their rarity but that they should not be on public display. (Two years earlier, during the final session of the Council of Trent, there was a drive to censure the Last Judgment of Michelangelo who was still alive at that time).

In the 18th century the popes once again proposed, withing a more organic frame of archeological information, the comparison with classical antiquity, particularly in comparison with Christian antiquity. This proposal had already been made to Clement XI (1700-21) in direct reference to epigraphic material and was realized by Benedict XIV (1740-58) and Clement XIII (1758-69) with the founding of the Apostolic Library Museums: the Sacred (1756) and the Profane (1767). The memorial stone of the Sacred Museum reads: "*ad augendum Urbis splendorem et asserendam religionis veritatem*". In the Treatise of Tolentino (1979) the Directory of the French Republic expressed a desire to have for its own capital city, Paris, those same work of art which graced that of Italy, Rome. All this shows the importance of this collection, the fruit of what is inappropiately referred to as the popes' collectionism. Among the first works to reach the Belvedere garden were: the Hermes statue called *Antinous*, the female portrait statue called *Venus Felix*, the *Torso*, and the *Sleeping Ariadne* (referred to during the Renaissance as Cleopatra). There were also the four statues of river divinities: the *Nile*, the *Tiber* (remained in Paris, part of Napoleon's booty), the *Tigris* and a fourth statue which is comparatively modest, in grey marble and which is now located in the Egyptian Museum.

Placed at the corners of the garden, these four rivers were explicit evocations of the Garden of Paradise; there, the so-called idols of Pius V were eloquently arranged in an aura of primeval innocence. The principal statues of this *hortulus* were valuable not only in terms of the development of

109. *The Belvedere Apollo*

110. The Laocoön group

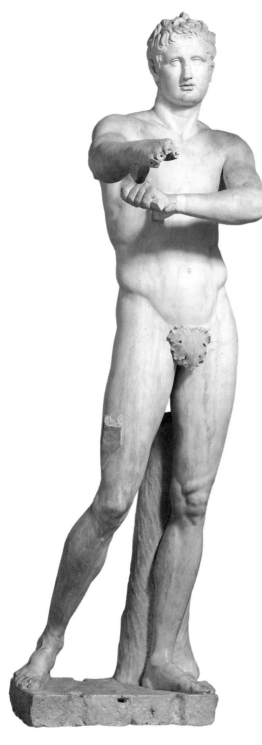

111. Statue of the Apoxyomenos

112. Statue of Hermes

Renaissance art and the art work of the following centuries, but also because they played an important role in the first reconstruction of the historical development of ancient art. The *Belvedere Apollo* is an excellent Roman replica from the Hadrian period of an original bronze work, attributed to Leochares, dating from the second half of the 4th century B.C. It is an ingenious interpretation of a divinity's epiphany. This elevated figure is master of the space surrounding him, for that space is dominated by his multidirectional gaze and position. This figure suggested to Michelangelo, the

113. The Belvedere Torso

intense torsion of Christ's head in the Last Judgment. Winckelmann said: ''the Apollo represents the highest ideal to be found among the ancient works of art that escaped destruction''. Winckelmann offered an inspired ideal reconstruction of the *Belvedere Torso*; while Michelangelo said of it: ''this is the work of a man that knew more than nature; it is a great misfortune that it is lost''. The sculptor of the Torso is the Athenian, Apollonius, son of Nestor who worked in the 1st century B.C.
An extraordinary charcoal sketch by Michelangelo, recently discovered under the New Sacristy of St.

114. Statue of the Tigris

115. Statue of the Nile

116. The sleeping Ariadne

Lorenzo in Florence, proves how much the artist was struck by the *Laocoön* group. That same sculpture was judged by Pliny the elder, during the reign of Emperor Titus (79-81 A.D.), to be superior to all other plastic and pictorial works of art known to him (*Naturalis Historia*, XXXVI, 37). It was Pliny who recorded the three sculptors from Rhodes who created that work: Hagesandros, Athanodoros and Polydoros. The original work dates between the second half of the 2nd century and the 1st century B.C. Let us now consider some of the last salient points in the development of the Papal collections. In 1604-05, the Roman fresco from the Augustan age (from the so-called third-style) was discovered on the Esquiline Hill; it was entitled the Aldobrandini Wedding after its first owner Pietro Aldobrandini. Based on a Hellenistic style, this fresco illustrates the preparations for a nuptial ceremony. Recovered and cleaned by Federico Zuccari, the story goes that this painting represented for painters what the Belvedere statues represented for sculptors. Consider Van Dyck's design, Rubens' admiration and the copies by both Pietro da Cortona and Nicol Poussin.

The most important moment in the life of the collection is now confronted: its conscious transformation into a museum. This phase coincides with the pontificates of Clement XIV (1769-74) and Pius VI (1775-99). They, particularly Pius VI who was already inspired by his predecessor, established a unified program. This program spanned from the brilliant job of the state financiary resources (in particular, from the Lottery), for acquiring ancient works of art, to the construction (by the architects Alessandro Dori and Michelangelo Simonetti) of buildings specifically created to be museum showplaces (the first of their kind in the Vatican), to Ennio Quirino Visconti's publication about the collection. Both the art works and their showplaces were disposed to fit into the already existent nucleus of the Belvedere and the Vatican Library. The framed garden became once again a courtyard, rendered octagonal by a protective loggia around the sides; while the loggia on the ground floor of the Palazzetto of Innocent VIII was changed into the luminous Statues' Gallery. The Rotunda, another room in the museum, is based on the Pantheon and houses the sculptures discovered during the Otricoli excavation directed by Pope Pius VI. The Room of the Muses is dedicated to a group of sculptures: precisely the nine *Muses*, with *Apollo Citaredo* and the many portraits of the Greek poets and philosophers. The Tommaso Conca frescoes decorate the vault of this

117. Venus Felix

118. Augustus of Prima Porta

119. View of the Round Room

121. View of the Room of the Muses

120. View of the Gregorian Profane Museum

room; this consciously-selected program is the neo-classical version of the theme expounded upon in the Room of the Liberal Arts, or in Raphael's Parnassus in the Segnatura. These are among the most convincing and pertinent tests of neo-classical architecture, the ancient aspect is kept alive in the structural rhythms, the colors and the spatial measurements. The statue of *Meleager* (already known in the 16th century) is greeted by this environment on its arrival in the Vatican. This is a 2nd century A.D. copy of an original statue dating from the 4th century B.C., linked with the name of Skopas, the Greek sculptor. The *Sauroktonos Apollo* arrived from the Palatine; the *Venus Cnidia* arrived from the Colonna Palace, Rome, and was placed in the Gabinetto delle Maschere, so-called because of the pavement mosaic originating from the Villa Adriana. In these last two works, based on original works by the acclaimed sculptor of antiquity, Praxiteles (active in the 4th century B.C.), the task of representing the olimpicity of a divinity is taken up with an audacious new language: a young Apollo absorbed in a cruel joke, yet without malice, Venus in a nudity that means inaccessibility to the glance.

122. Relief with the monogram of Christ

The Christian Museum, founded by Pius IX (1846-78) in 1854 in the Lateran Palace two years before the institution of the Commission of Sacred Archeology, was transferred into the newest Vatican museum (by the Passarelli Studio, 1965-71) at the behest of Pope John XXIII.

Displayed in that museum by Giuseppe Marchi and Giovan Battista de Rossi are the finds from the catacombs that could not be conserved *in situ*. The above-mentioned Commission was in charge of the excavation of those catacombs and held the responsibility for the finds. Maturing with the progress of archeological science, we see a critical detachment from the ancient works, even at the cost of losing that unification obtained by the Christian culture's suggesting or imposing its particular values on all antiquity; a detachment which demonstrates the need for a more concrete, objective and articulate presence of specific Paleochristian evidence in the museum.

123. Statue of the Good Shepherd

124. Sarcophagus with the Adoration of the Magi

125. Sarcophagus with the Good Shepherd and the apostles

126. Sarcophagus with the monogram of Christ

On October 27, 1932, Pius XI inaugurated the definitive seat of the Vatican Picture Gallery in a building (by Luca Beltrami) near the monumental entrance which that same year saw the "opening" of the Vatican museums on Rome. Such a typically lay and modern institution, where the museum element appears all the more arid when we recall the function and natural environment of such objects as a portrait or an altarpiece, could never have been born in the Vatican without the influence exerted by external circumstances. This indeed proves to be the case. In 1815 the Vienna Congress sanctioned the restitution of those paintings stolen by Napoleon (according to the Treatise of Tolentino) to the Pontifical State, the churches and convents of Rome; the Congress made one stipulation: that these paintings be accessible in Italy to the public. The paintings, therefore, did not return to their previous domains, but were relocated: Raphael's *Transfiguration*, once in the church of St. Peter in Montorio, is now in the Salon of Raphael in the Pinacoteca; it hangs beside the *Madonna*

127. Giotto, the Stefaneschi Triptych

of Foligno, which once hung in the so-called Chiesa delle Contesse in Foligno. This phenomen gave rise to what might be termed as the popes' induced collectionism. From Pope Gregory XVI to Pius IX, the popes directed the acquisitions and changes made in the Picture Gallery, such as the removal of Giotto's *Stefaneschi Triptych* from the Sala del Capitolo, where it had been since 1931, to the Picture Gallery. That painting, dated around 1315, was originally intended for the main altar of St. Peter's in Rome.

The Borgia Apartment, having been neglected for many years, was the first seat of the new Picture Gallery. The roamings began five years later and were halted one century later by Pius XI. First, the third floor of the Gregorian Loggias, then the Tapestries' Gallery, then the Apartment of St. Pius V, then that of Gregory XIII, and once again, under the pontificate of Pius X, the east arm of the Belvedere Courtyard. An eloquent history of perplexities, generated by this museum creature wanting

128. *Melozzo da Forlì, Sixtus IV and Platina*

129. *Leonardo da Vinci, St. Jerome*

130. *Raphael, Transfiguration*

131. Raphael, Madonna of Foligno

132. Brussel's Manufacture, tapestry with the Miraculous
draught of fishes (from Raphael's cartoon)

133. Titian, Madonna of the Frari

134. Federico Barocci, Rest on the Flight into Egypt

135. Caravaggio, Deposition

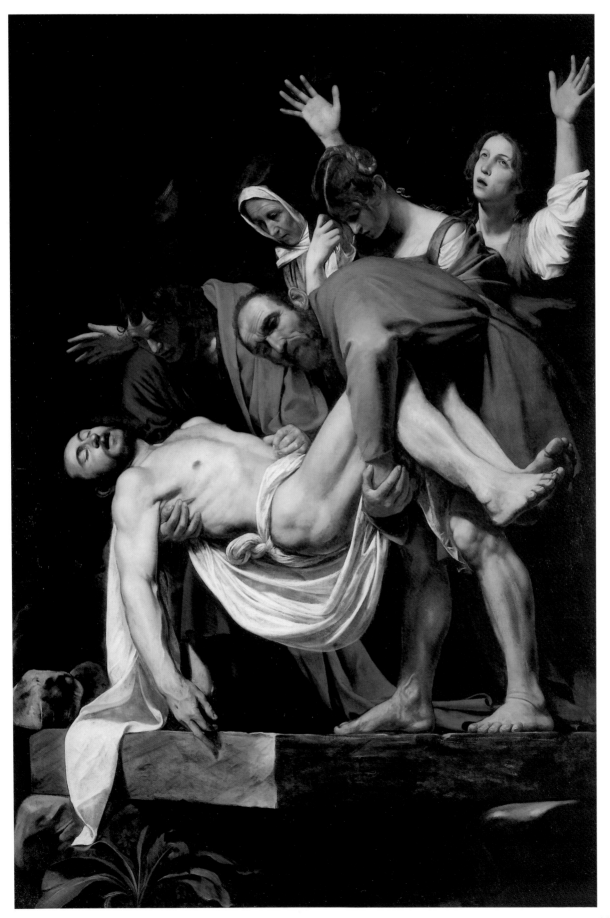

in roots (later the Lateran Collection and the Byzantine Icon Collection). It is indeed significant that it was Pius XI (1922-39), the cultured and active protagonist of many other events still to be considered, who was responsible for many courageous cuts with the past and projects for the future, on behalf of the Church. He too realized the situation and established the Picture Gallery, as suggested by the Vienna Congress, in the Vatican Museums. Let us now consider some of the more important works that these stories have brought to mind, and that are on show in the fifteen rooms of the Picture Gallery, in chronological order and according to the school. First is the already cited *Stefaneschi Triptych*; depicted in this work by Giotto and assistants (circa 1315) are an enthroned Christ and the martyrdom of St. Peter and St. Paul. There are identifiable topographical elements included in this work, such as the *meta romuli*, an ancient monument which that artist had surely seen near the Constantine Basilica when he visited it during a pilgrimage called by Boniface VIII in celebration of the First Jubilee. Let us also recall the fresco (1477) painted by Melozzo da Forlì, located in the old library of Sixtus IV; it represents the *Nomination of Bartolomeo Platina* as the first Prefect of the library. Raphael's Transfiguration is indisputably the most important work in the Picture Gallery. Commissioned by Cardinal Giulio dei Medici in 1517 for Narbonne Cathedral, Raphael had nearly completed the work when he died in 1520. So lamenting his premature death (everything had been precocious in his existence), Raphael's contemporaries may have assisted in creating the fame of that painting as an unfinished work, a belief that has been proven false by a recent restoration. The very powerful painting by Leonardo (1480) of a penitent *St. Jerome* is indeed an unfinished work. The incomplete state in which one finds this work allows one to analyse the artist-scientist who through the gestures, anatomy and facial expression of that emaciated figure, enquires into the setting in which and the means by which the old hermit attained an elevated spiritual state. We shall conclude with Titian's altarpiece—opulent Venetian color and thick impasto—painted in 1528 for the Venetian church of San Nicolò dei Frari; and also with Caravaggio's *Deposition from the Cross* painted in 1604 for the New Church in Rome. The rapport between the bodies struck by light and the just-perceivable presences in half-light, the crescendo that grows from the rigid stone, the weighty body of Christ to the absorbed sorrow and weakness of the Virgin and the Magdalene, climaxing in the gesture of the crying figure depicted above; all reminds us, in the ingeniousness of the baroque invention, just how far along this path of research Raphael was in his *Transfiguration*.

The words of Leo X, herein recorded, were quasireiterated by Paul VI in his May 7th speech to the artists gathered in the Sistine Chapel. Paul VI, reopening the colloquy with contemporary art, (a colloquy which later materialised with the opening on 23 June, 1937 of the Gallery of Modern Religious Art) said with underlined frankness: ''Art and beauty and even worse in our eyes, the cult of God have been poorly served'', because lately the Church's recourse has been to the ''surrogates'' of art, to the imitations and to ''oleography''. He continues: ''These are the reasons for which our ministry has sought you''. Paul's project was farsighted and broad, it was neither restricted nor pretentious. Contemporary art was well-received and physical hospitality was offered, in the form of the Apostolic Palace (in fact the lesser known more ancient part of the Palace—between the Borgia Apartment and the area below the Sistine Chapel—was given for this purpose). At a distance of but a few years we see that this move has become a symbol of the desire to offer ideal hospitality, without stipulations, to a new art form embracing values affirmed by the Church. Nothing greater would be possible today, considering the recent crises that have arisen between the individual and culture, between the handed-down values and personal and social ethics and between the artist and society; such facts point to the specific crises suffered by the relationship between the Church and Art, between a committee that presents its ideas and a research art that refracts from those ideas and finally, between a committee viewing the ''functionality'' of Art and Art that does not want or does not know how to bear the burden of ''direction''. In short an art bearing the mark of doubt, as

136. View of a room of the Collection of Modern Religious Art

perhaps it had never done before, is invited to answer the call of revelation and preaching, to examine it thoroughly to confront it. The artist was not compelled to create "sacred" art, art with liturgical distinction. (Such work was, however, very much present in the new collection: consider Matisse's Rosary Chapel of Vence, Lucio Fontana's sketches for the door of the Milan Cathedral, Giacomo Manzù's furnishings for the Chapel of Peace). This is a striking concession to the personal, psychological-intimist vein of so much contemporary art: daughter of the bourgeois revolutions. However, a precise function may be seen in the wish of Paul VI that "a new artistic tradition surface from this first religious modern art collection, located next to, though not to be set in comparison with, the surrounding Vatican masterpieces, and that it establishes in the artists' hearts the conviction that the Catholic Church. . ., honoring the work exhibited there . . ., awaits the flowering of a new spring of post-conciliary religious art''.

The passage across which the treasures of Humanism flowed during the 15th and 16th centuries, breaking the golden circle of the medieval Christian culture and renewing the language of the Church in, more simply, a figurative sense, is re-opened today, almost *ex-cathedra*, with respect and faith. The collection initially contained more than seven hundred works by two hundred and fifty different artists, for the most part living; these works were distributed throughout more than fifty rooms. The collection is continually growing because of the donations made by the owners of the works or by the artists themselves.

137. Lucio Fontana, bronze portrait of Martin V

It would seem contrary to the spirit of the collection (and the aims of this album) if at this point we were to isolate quotations, or if we were to select masterpieces. It will suffice to note the gamut of responses that the founder of the collection received. Let us recall the presence there of the religious, or rather Christian, work by Georges Rouault, the most dramatic exponent of the French Catholic experience to which the spirituality of Paul VI was closely linked. There is a turn to the religious, not promoted by expressed conviction, but by respect and affection. A bronze portrait sculpture of Pope John was the consequence of the rapport between that pope and the sculptor Giacomo Manzù, and the Chapel of Peace similarly materialized due to the collaboration between Manzù and Giuseppe de Luca. There is also, at the other end of the scale, Francis Bacon's study Velasquez's Innocent X: a bitter disintegration of a portrait, an anguished caricature of power.

138. Giacomo Manzù, bust of John XXIII

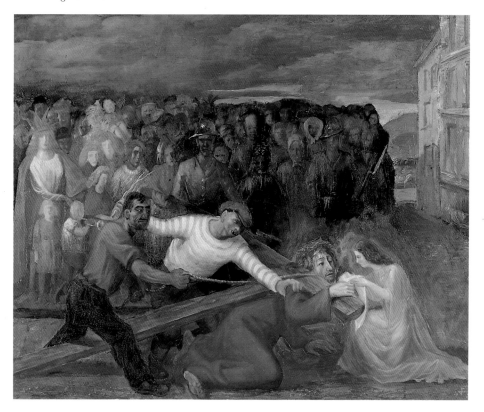

139. Otto Dix, the Ascent to Calvary

140. Graham Sutherland, Crucifixion

141. *Mask from the New Guinea*

142. *African mask*

The *Acts of St. Thomas*, purportedly a Syrian text dating back to the 3rd century, tells us that in Jerusalem the apostles divided among themselves those areas to which they would "go and preach to all people" (Mathew 28:18-20). Thomas was given India where, after having evangelized the southwest part (the "Christians of St Thomas", or Syrian-Malabrians), he was martyred. Thus, while Saul, the ex-persecutioner of Christians, was becoming the evangelist of western pagans, the "one who doubted Christ", became the pioneer of the eastern apostolic itinerary, that same route which centuries later was to see the Missions of Preachers and of the Minor Brothers (from the 13th to the 14th centuries), of the Capuchin and of the Jesuits (from the 16th to the 17th centuries). In 1622, Gregory XV established an organization, capable of answering in an organic and unified manner those intrusions made by the European Powers into selected missionaries, called the Sacred Congregation *De Propaganda Fide*. Three centuries later, in 1923, Pius XI—the pontiff who was later to define the reduction of the Church's territorial sovereignty to the symbolic dimensions of the State of the Vatican City—reactivated the missionary activities of the Church on better cognitive, scientific and practical bases. On April 24, 1923, he decided to exhibit in Rome "all that could possibly serve to illustrate the missions of the entire Catholic orb: their activities, the places where these activities are exercised and their works".

144. *Mask Aruacos from Colombia*

145. *Statue of the god Tu from the Polynesia*

147. *Chinese statuette of a groom*

146. *Statue of the Mexican god Quetzalcoatl*

This was to occur during the Holy Year of 1925. That Missionary Exhibition, in preparation for which the most capillary ganglions of the Catholic presence in the world were mobilized, took place between December 21, 1924 and January 10, 1926. It received more than one million visitors. At the official closing, the Pope promised that the contents of the exhibition would be placed in a new museum to be called the Ethnological Missionary Museum. Located in the Lateran Palace, this museum opened on December 21, 1927. At the behest of John XXIII, the museum was closed to the public on February 1, 1963 and re-opened in its new Vatican location (work of the Passarelli Studio) in 1973. It holds a considerable patrimony of approximately forty thousand objects and groups of objects: evidence of all the civilisations touched by the missionaries of the Church. All is arranged in an irreplaceable picture: a story of great, ardent individuals, of *societates peregrinantium pro Cristo*, sometimes of an apostolate instrumentalized by political colonialisms, of a civilization now respectful of indigenous languages, now strongly westernized. It is not only a historical-religious panorama of the most disparate cultures, though this is its most relevant aspect, but it is also a panorama of the popular traditions of the extra-European world.

143. *The Hut of the Spirits from the New Guinea*

148. *The pontifical gala carriages*

149. *The car of Pius XII*

150. The helicoidal staircase at the entrance to the Vatican Museums

With the Carriage Museum, also opened in 1973, our travels near their end. Instituted by Paul VI in 1963, in a large area under the Framed Garden, the museum houses a stupendous collection of carriages used by popes and cardinals for pleasure, travel, the semi-gala, the gala and the grand gala: Leo XIII's carriage, so like a vehicle from a fairytale, the noble black landaus used by Pius XI, and also a small model of the jet which transported Paul VI to the United Nations.

The establishment of the Vatican City State, following the ratification of the Lateran Treaty (1929), admitted the Vatican Museums into the new organism as a central state office, affording them the title of Monuments, Museums and Papal Galleries (a regulation dating from 5 December, 1932). The urban structure of the City State, its exigencies of internal autonomy and the duties connected with the presentation of the cultural and artistic patrimony to the public, directed Pius XI to build a new entrance to the museum: ''shorter and more practicable from the city''. The location for this entrance could not be placed in any other spot than at the southern-most extremity of the state, the closest point to the bastions, but also at the point where there is the greatest difference of level between the interior and the exterior. The Renaissance (the period which the Lombard artists of Pius XI's pontificate imitated in each of their works) was immediately cited at the outset and without any half measures: statues by Raphael and Michelangelo are located near the tympanum of the entrance, and the monumental stairway, with its double helicoidal ramp (Giuseppe Momo, 1932), wich overcomes the rise of sixteen meters in ninety-eight meters, is reminiscent of St. Patrick's Well in Orvieto by Sangallo. The new entrance was inaugurated on January 2, 1933, and soon became the most heavily travelled passageway of this minute state.

THE VATICAN GARDENS

Behind the entrance of the Vatican Museums, studding the fourty-four acres of Vatican land, lie towards the south: the Picture Gallery, the Academy of Sciences in the enlarged lodge of Pius IV, the Palace of the Governatorato, the Studio del Mosaico and the railway station; towards the west: the Vatican Radio; further east: the industrial center, the Post Offices, the Polyglot Typography, seat of the *Osservatore Romano*. Lilliputian offices or powerful representative seats, the workshops of Pius XI are all characterised by a grandiose tone in harmony not only with the grace of the surrounding Italian-style gardens, embelleshied by the fountains by Giovanni Vasanzio, with the ancient buildings which reach as far as the western limit of the Vatican lands, but also in harmony with the universal theater on which Pius XI wished to base this small Sovereign State, envisaged as a spring compressed within the Leonine walls. Just how well the actual interpretation of the ministry of Peter's Successor coincides with what that pontiff had previously planned, amid the threatening clouds of the Second World War, then advancing with great speed, is before the eyes of all to see.

154

155

156. *Fountain of the Eagle*

157. *Fountain of the Galley*

158. *Interiour court of the Casina of Pius IV*

159. *House of the Gardener and statue of St. Peter from the dome*

160. *Government Palace*

LIST OF ARTISTS